THE HISTORY OF THE WHITE HOUSE

MALLARD PRESS

Photography
Bettmann Archive
FPG International
National Portrait Gallery, Smithsonian Institution.
National Archives, Washington, D.C.
Odyssey Publishing Ltd.
Prints Old and Rare.

Photo Researcher
Leora Kahn

Photo Editor
Annette Lerner

MALLARD PRESS

An imprint of BDD Promotional Book Company Inc., 666 Fifth Avenue, New York, NY 10103

Mallard Press and its accompanying design and logo are trademarks of BDD Promotional Book Company, Inc.

Color separations by Advance Laser Graphic Arts, Hong Kong.

Printed and bound by Leefung Asco Ltd., Hong Kong.

ISBN 0 7924 5489 8

Previous page: an early view of the White House. Amid all the formality, President and Mrs. Bush (right) manage relaxed smiles as they wave goodbye to President Mikhail Gorbachev and his wife at the end of their 1990 stay at the White House.

1792 – Irish-born architect James Hoban wins a design contest for the president's house over a field of competitors including Thomas Jefferson. He is presented a gold medal worth $500 and accepts an offer to superintend its building. Cornerstone is laid four months later.

1800 – President John Adams moves into the still-unfinished house. His wife Abigail makes do, though she complains that "not one room or chamber is finished of the whole" and that "promises are all you can obtain." The Adamses fit out the upstairs oval room for weekly formal receptions, while laundry is hung to dry in the audience room.

1801 – President Thomas Jefferson takes up residence and installs furnishings gathered in Paris during his years as Minister to France. He also hires a French chef and upgrades the presidential wine cellar. A widower, he turns the job of official hostess over to Dolley Madison, the wife of his friend and Virginia neighbor, James Madison.

1805 – James Madison Randolph, the seventh child of Jefferson's daughter, Martha, is the first child born in the Presidential Mansion.

1810 – An article in the newspaper *The Baltimore Whig* calls the mansion the "White House" for the first time. Its white sandstone exterior makes it stand out among the brick houses that are common in Washington.

1814 – British troops set fire to Washington's public buildings, including the White House. Heavy rain extinguishes the flames, but all that remains are charred exterior walls.

1817 – President James Monroe moves into the reconstructed mansion, bringing his own furnishings complemented with pieces imported from France.

1820 – Monroe's daughter, Maria, marries Samuel Gouverneur in the first White House wedding.

1829 – President Andrew Jackson invites the people to celebrate his inauguration in his new home. Some 20,000 crash through the gates.

1841 – William Henry Harrison dies within a month of becoming President and the is first to lie in state in the East Room.

1850 – President Millard Fillmore has a modern kitchen installed, replacing the open fireplaces that served his predecessors. His wife, Abigail, lobbies Congress to furnish the house with books after being shocked to find there is not even a dictionary there.

1864 – Armed officers of the Washington police force are assigned to guard the life of a president for the first time following threats against Lincoln.

1869 – Julia Dent Grant, wife of the new president, refuses to move into the White House because of its shabby condition. Congress responds with funds for renovation and decoration in the fashionable Greek style.

1877 – Rutherford B. Hayes and his wife, Lucy, ban drinking in the White House. A social historian records, "water flowed like wine." The President has the mansion's first telephone installed. Lucy begins the tradition of Easter egg rolling on the lawn.

1881 – President James A. Garfield has an elevator installed.

1881 – President Chester A. Arthur auctions off twenty-four wagonloads of furnishings and moves elsewhere while workmen directed by Louis Comfort Tiffany redecorate the White House.

1886 – Grover Cleveland is the first President married in the White House. John Philip Sousa and the Marine Band play the wedding march.

1892 – Benjamin Harrison's wife, Mary, calls for expansion of the White House, but settles for extermination of rats, replacement of rotting floors, modernization of kitchens and greenhouses and electric lights. The house celebrates its centennial.

1902 – Theodore Roosevelt hires the architectural firm of McKim, Mead & White to rebuild the White House interior and to replace the greenhouses with an office wing, including the first press room. The President makes the name "White House" official by adding it to his personal stationery.

1909 – William Howard Taft expands the West Pavillion to create the Oval Office. As the first president to use automobiles, he replaces the stables with a garage.

1929 – Fire damages the Executive Offices, forcing President Herbert Hoover and his staff to relocate.

1934 – Franklin D. Roosevelt rebuilds the West Wing, adding an underground Cabinet Room and a swimming pool. East Wing is rebuilt later in the Roosevelt Administration and office space is provided for his wife, Eleanor.

1945 – During construction of a second-floor porch, it is discovered that the structure of the house has deteriorated dangerously. President Harry Truman orders complete rebuilding from the cellar up following original designs, adding steel beams for structural strength.

1961 – First Lady Jacqueline Kennedy forms the Fine Arts Commission to renovate the White House reflecting the history of the presidents and their families.

In 1790 George Washington (facing page top left) fixed upon a date for the Federal Government's eventual move to the city that bears his name. By the "first Monday in December 1800," the date designated by Washington, his successor John Adams (facing page top right) was installed in the still-unfinished mansion. Each occupant of the White House has adapted the rooms. The Red Room (right), initially used as an antechamber for the Cabinet Room or the President's Library, was converted into a music room in the late nineteenth century. Facing page bottom: groups of people wait in the lobby of the White House to petition the President.

A competition to design the Executive Mansion was organized in 1792. The winning design, submitted by Irishman James Hoban, fulfilled the commissioners' desire for "a grandeur of conception, a Republican simplicity, and ... true Elegance of proportion." The decision to build the portico and curved steps onto the south side of the building (these pages), as envisaged in Hoban's original design, was taken by Thomas Jefferson, but the work was not completed until 1825.

Historical pictures depict the grounds of the White House as picturesque, but some people considered them less than pleasant because of the foul smell from a nearby canal. Constitution Avenue was created when the canal was covered over in 1827.

The arrival of President Buchanan and his niece Harriet Lane at the White House marked the beginning of a period of entertaining that was comparable with that of a European court.

Since the time of Thomas Jefferson, representatives from the major Indian tribes (left) had been invited to the White House from time to time to meet with the President in an attempt to allay their fears, relieve tensions, and create ties. Tensions of another sort exploded in 1861 when the southern states sought to secede from the Union. On July 4, 1861, just a few weeks before they were to march to Charleston, Union troops under the leadership of General Sandford (below) were reviewed by President Abraham Lincoln (right) outside the White House.

President Grant (left), surrounded by members of his Cabinet, prepares to leave the White House for his second inauguration. Accompanied by the music of the Marine Band of the Navy Yard, nineteenth-century Washingtonians (facing page) enjoy a Saturday-afternoon stroll in the grounds of the White House.

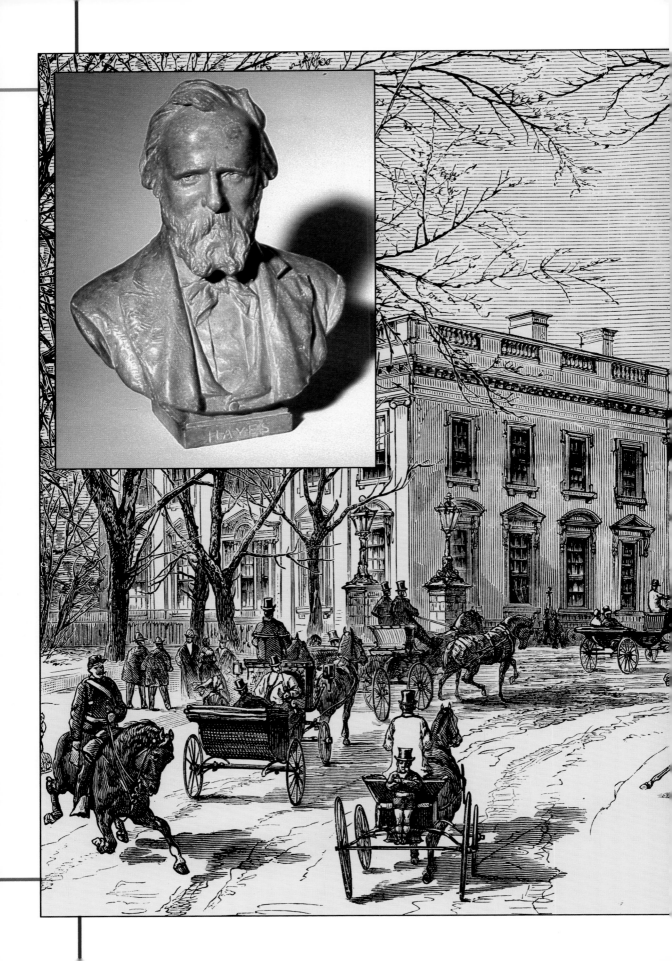

Although horse-drawn carriages (left) outside the mansion in 1877 give an air of normality, the early days of the Hayes administration were, in reality, marked by fears of a coup d'état. Rutherford B. Hayes (above left), following a closely-run election, took the oath in secrecy at the White House two days before his formal inauguration.

"Elegant Arthur" (facing page), a widower, managed to evade the schemes of Washington matchmakers. His own plans for the White House were more successful. He auctioned wagonloads of unwanted furniture and called in Louis Tiffany to give the mansion a face-lift. In the Cross Hall, a stained-glass screen, Tiffany's most famous addition, gave some privacy from office seekers (right).

Crowds of people gather in the gardens of the White House. Today's neatly manicured lawns are a long way from the litter-strewn ones of the past.

Although an increased administrative workload and greater staff numbers had long required more space in the White House, work on a wing to house the executive offices did not get under way until the presidency of Theodore Roosevelt (above left). Sadly, much of this 1902 construction was destroyed by a fire on Christmas Eve, 1929. During its reconstruction both Herbert Hoover (above right) and Franklin D. Roosevelt (left) worked, as earlier presidents had, from the White House proper. The White House expanded upward as well as outward. In 1927, Hoban's original but long-postponed third story added a further eighteen rooms, while the rebuilding of the West Wing (facing page) in 1934 created extra underground working space.

The Yellow Oval Room was filled with items from his private collection by Franklin D. Roosevelt and used as a study. The Roosevelt's furnishings, said to resemble "an old and ultrarespectable summer resort hotel," brought a homely atmosphere to the mansion.

The tradition of blue decor in the "elliptical saloon," the masterpiece of Hoban's design, originated in the presidency of Van Buren. In 1934, during the reconstruction of the West Wing, the Blue Room (facing page) was transformed into President Roosevelt's office, and its usual furnishings made way for the President's desk. The flag of the United States and the Presidential flag remained in their customary places on either side of the desk despite the change in location. Roosevelt's enthusiasm for sailing ships is reflected in the collection of prints he hung on the walls of the "Monroe Room" (right). Below: the White House kitchen in 1935, before it was modernized.

The carved, marble mantel in the Green Room (facing page), above which hangs David Martin's portrait of Benjamin Franklin, is one of a pair ordered by James Monroe. Both mantels, separated in the 1902 renovation, previously stood in the State Dining Room. A suite of Bellangé furniture, with the American eagle woven into the upholstery, was another of Monroe's acquisitions, and was bought for the Blue Room (below). It was then auctioned off by Buchanan, and all but three of the pieces currently in the room are replicas. Constant renovation left its mark on the White House. So serious were the findings of the 1948 structural investigation that President Truman (left) moved in to nearby Blair House.

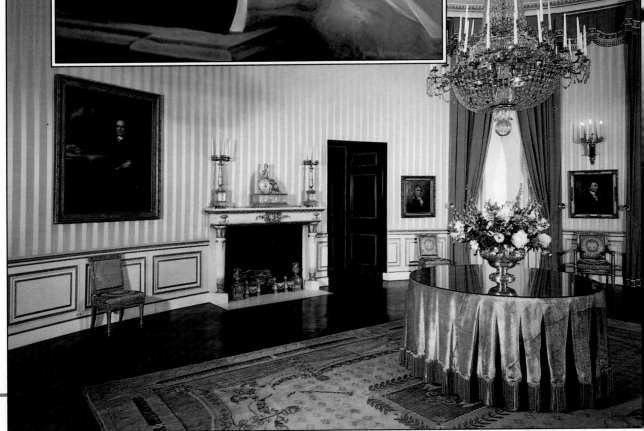

President Fillmore's wife, a former schoolteacher, persuaded Congress of the need for a library in the White House. The books purchased with the $5,000 appropriated by Congress, were initially housed in the Yellow Oval Room, but were moved to their present ground-floor location (facing page bottom) in 1937. The State Dining Room (facing page top) was enlarged in 1902 when the stairway in the Cross Hall was removed. This made it possible to hold larger state receptions. Kennedy (right) speaks to the American people from the Oval Office after his return from his 1961 European trip.

The East Room, used by Abigail Adams as a place to dry her laundry, has since been the scene of important political and cultural events. In 1961 it was the setting for the swearing-in of President Kennedy's new cabinet.

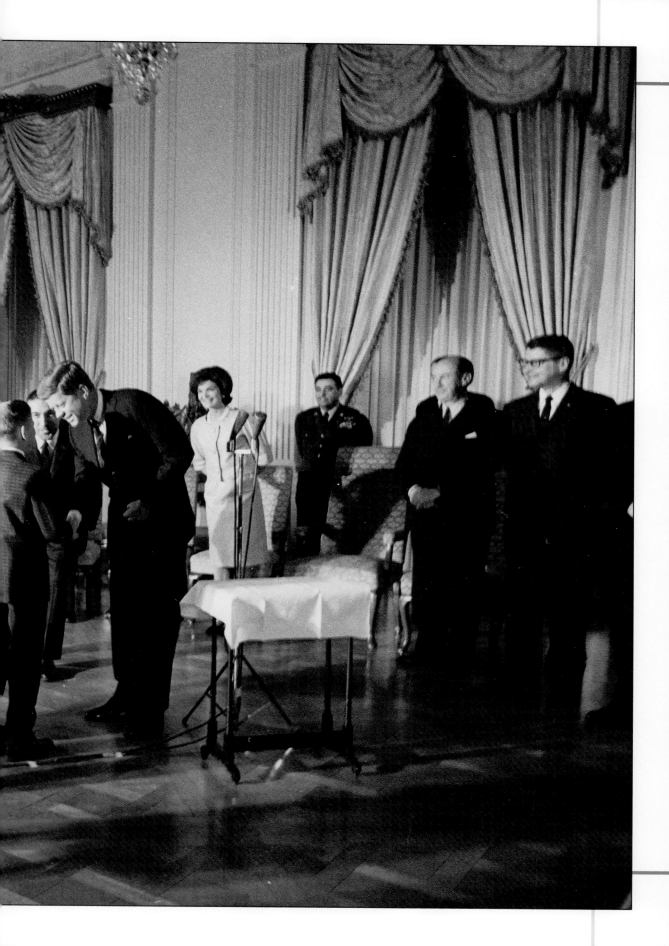

The Kennedy children, Caroline and John Junior (facing page top), enliven the somber atmosphere of the Oval Office by dancing for their father. The Kennedy era saw innovations in protocol such as the Welcoming Ceremony. The presidential helicopter (facing page) was introduced by Eisenhower, and used to bring newly-arrived guests to the White House for the ceremony. This tradition has now been dropped, and guests are brought to the mansion by car. Republican Richard Nixon (facing page bottom), beaten by John Kennedy in the election of 1960, became President in 1969.

The National Portrait Gallery, Smithsonian Institution

The Presidential seal decorating the front of the lectern from which Reagan delivers his speech of welcome to King Fahd of Saudi Arabia (above) is one of the emblems of office. Left: the mansion's magnificent north facade can be seen beyond the statue of Andrew Jackson.

The ornate American Victorian furniture that characterizes the Lincoln Bedroom (below) was installed by Truman. Now used for guests, the room bears little resemblance to the cluttered office that Lincoln knew. During the Civil War the elegant East Room (facing page) was occupied by Union soldiers. Intended as a "Public Audience Room," the classically-decorated East Room is the most formal of the reception rooms. The room's magnificent Steinway piano with eagle-shaped supports was donated by its New-York-based manufacturer. Other examples of fine American craftsmanship can be seen in the Map Room (right). The "blockfront" style of the chest and slant top desk was developed by American cabinetmakers from the Chippendale style.

Beneath a portrait of George Washington, President Bush and the Soviet leader Mikhail Gorbachev (facing page) prepare for the 1990 summit. At the height of the arms race, when the threat of war between the Soviet Union and the United States was ever present, such a series of meetings seemed inconceivable. Above: President Reagan meets with Nobel Peace Prize winner Mother Teresa. Right: President and Mrs. Bush photographed with Benazir Bhutto, then President of Pakistan and her husband Asif Ali Zardari.

The swampy, malarial land surrounding the White House was still covered with shacks and workmen's tools when the John and Abigail Adams, the White House's first inhabitants, arrived. From this inauspicious beginning, attractive, landscaped gardens (these pages) have been created. The Spring Garden Tour (overleaf) is particularly popular with visitors to the White House. The eighteen-acre estate becomes a mass of color as the garden's flowering trees burst into life. When framed by cherry and magnolia blossom, the sandstone White House is perhaps at its most beautiful.